FRENCH COUNTRY COTTAGE
Inspired Gatherings

FRENCH COUNTRY COTTAGE
Inspired Gatherings

COURTNEY ALLISON

GIBBS SMITH
TO ENRICH AND INSPIRE HUMANKIND

For my mom, whose love of home and entertaining has shown me from a young age that creating a welcoming place for friends and family to gather also creates wonderful memories that last long after the occasion.

My memories of those childhood occasions have encouraged me to create gatherings for my own family, who inspire me every day.

CONTENTS

INTRODUCTION

GATHERINGS. IT IS A WORD THAT BRINGS TO MIND SOMETHING WONDERFUL. Something full of excitement and anticipation and inspiration. Lots of laughs, special conversations, meaningful moments, and memories in the making.

Inspired gatherings with friends and family—whether small and intimate or full of guests and energy—are food for the soul.

From the time I was a young girl, I remember being quite enamored with anything to do with gatherings, from dinner parties to lakeside getaways with family and friends to Thanksgiving dinner at my grandmother's house in the mountains. There was something about those special times that held a certain fascination for me, even when I was little. When I knew that there was a special occasion coming up on the calendar, I got a little bit giddy with the anticipation, knowing what was sure to be an enchanted event was just around the corner.

Though I wasn't involved in the aspects of party planning, packing for a getaway with the family, or the basic details of what goes on behind the scenes, the appeal for me started with the simplest of things: a notepad and pen that mother would use to jot down things to remember and the smallest of details she didn't want to overlook. She would plan everything, right down to when the invitations would go out and what time in the evening the candles would be lit.

The hors d'oeuvres. The dinner. The beverages. The desserts. They were all there, of course, but beyond those handwritten notes and list of nibbles were the things that delighted me most. The candles. The Christmas tree twinkles. The music playing in the background. The way the sun dropped behind the trees at a particular time and the stage that had been set for the party felt like it came to life. Along with all this came the laughter of guests and the smile that my mother wore when she could finally take a moment to relax and enjoy the moment.

Now that I am older, I think back to our gatherings when planning and hosting my own, and while I have vivid memories of the elements and layers that went into each one, the china patterns, the tablecloths, and the particular food are not what stand out to me. It is much more the feelings, sights, sounds, smells, and ambience of the gatherings that have stayed with me. That sweet smell of my grandmother's fudge that you could almost taste from the moment you stepped in through her front door for Thanksgiving dinner. The crisp mountain air and smell of smoke from the campfire at the lake and & the feeling of the scratchy wool camping blankets. The burst of yellow and pink wild flowers gathered up from the garden and placed on the table for a summer evening barbecue.

It seems our family has a long line of entertaining women who had scratch pads filled with lists, notes with tidbits to remember stuck to the counters, and old favorite recipes earmarked in the ruffled pages of cookbooks. Those formerly secret family recipes handwritten on old recipe cards were spotted with flour and oil stains, evidence of how many times they had been used over the years.

My mom was always planning the next great get-together, whether it was a grand occasion, like a block party, or something simple, like a picnic dinner at the ocean. My grandmother was much the same in her love of entertaining and having a house full of people. No doubt she was an influence on my mom, just as Nana, my great-grandmother, was on her.

The same dishes that my grandmother used—the ones covered in pink flowers and lace details—are in my cupboard for everyday occasions now, and whenever we bring them out to use them, I am reminded of those Thanksgivings and Easters at her house and the memories that come along with them.

Though holiday gatherings were some of the most memorable, I also loved the simplest of get-togethers. The tailgate meet-ups at the drive-in theater in high school. The summer barbecue in the backyard with childhood friends. The summer weeks we spent staying on Lake Tahoe with three other families, and the weekends skiing, where I mostly looked forward to sitting by the fire and warming my frozen fingers and frostbitten cheeks.

Gatherings are not just tables and lavish occasions. They are the beach picnics in the sunshine and salty ocean air and quiet camping trips at the Russian River, complete with all the layers of thick, plaid cotton sleeping bags, campfire stories, and evenings lying cozy next to the fire staring at star-filled skies and talking until we fall asleep.

There is something about those moments. That simple in-between feeling when it seems the world stops for a few minutes while you look around at people making sweet memories. It is inspiring to think that something as simple as a quiet morning on the lake sipping cocoa can become a long-lasting memory for someone.

Today I am just as inspired whenever I am creating a beautiful gathering. I have learned that a dinner party is much more than a grand dining table set with elegant china and flatware, layers of flowers, and beautiful twinkling ambience. It is a time to be together. To break bread over an evening simmered in conversation, where laughter flows freely and friendships and moments fill you up more than the food. I often find myself pausing in the busyness of the evening to soak up each element and layer. The music, the sound of the crickets, the hearty laughs, and muted conversations. The candles flickering and burning low as the clock moves closer to midnight. The smell of dessert warming in the oven and the joyful smiles on the faces of friends all around.

To me, a gathering is much more than a party or an event. It is kindred souls coming together to share an experience that is full of inspired moments where many small and big memories are made.

ELEMENTS
AND LAYERS

Much like design, where one thing is complementary to another, my essentials for any gathering that I am planning take a very similar approach. There is, of course, the unexpected in the mix of accoutrements. And there is the *pièce de résistance*, that one thing in any setting that the gathering simply won't feel the same without: it is that sprinkle of magic, the ambience.

Creating that ambience is key, and it is the first thing that I start with when planning any get-together. Ambience is a layer of factors that create the mood: for example, the candles flickering on the table. The twinkle lights hanging in the tree branches. The music playing in the background. The flowers. The crumble and crunch of the bread as you take a bite. It is all of the sensory elements that bring your event to life and make it an experience to remember—the sights, sounds, feelings, and even the taste of the gathering.

Each layer could stand alone and make a statement by itself, but when you put them all together and find yourself with that delightful mishmash, that is where the magic happens. And that is my most favorite thing about planning a gathering of any kind.

Have you ever looked at an image and instantly imagined what it would be like to be transported there? To feel the crisp air on your skin, to breathe it in and notice the nuances in the scent? That feeling of the warmth of the candles flickering on your face, the taste of the dessert as it melts in your mouth, the sounds of laughter amidst the music playing softly in the background?

Those elements are all part of an experience that your senses will remember long after the evening is wrapped up. It is much like an old familiar song that comes on the radio and instantly transports you back to when you first heard it twenty years ago—and you remember exactly where you were and what you were doing.

That ambience and experience is something that I want guests to remember for years and years to come.

Creating Layers on the Table

Think of your table as part of the story of your occasion. Each layer on your table is another piece of the puzzle—another detail, big or small, and another opportunity to create an evening that guests will remember long after the candles have burned down and the last bite of dessert has been enjoyed.

When designing the table, the first thing to consider is the type of event you are putting together. Is it a formal one—something at a table with the seating arrangement indicated by place cards? Or is it a casual affair, where people will grab their plates and settle in where they feel comfortable?

Now that you are thinking of the general direction, you can plan the place settings, including the dishes you will use, which flatware adds the touch you are going for, and which stemware will be a perfect fit.

A rule I tend to follow: other than the most formal gatherings, which is where I love to indulge in the most luxurious layers on the table, I tend to use gathered, mismatched stemware and flatware for most occasions. I think imperfect or unmatched place settings make guests feel more at ease.

The Place Settings

Choose your place settings based on the occasion. Will it be elegant, or will a casual setting support the mood you want to create? You don't need china or chargers for every table; simple is best sometimes. For a more formal event, layering dishes—the charger, dinner plate, salad plate, and bread plate—is a beautiful and inspired way to set the table, even if it is just for two.

Something to think about while choosing your table accessories: the place settings are an area where you can really create your personal touch. They can be statement makers with decadent details, or they can add a subtle elegance with vintage floral and embossed china from yesteryear.

For something formal, start with a charger and add several detailed plates to build a delicious stack of china. Then top with a linen napkin and modern gold flatware. Paired with chunky goblets, this type of look is elegant. For a less formal occasion, your everyday best plates, gathered-up vintage china plates, or even basic white dishes paired with vintage napkins and collected silver flatware will make a pretty table.

Vintage china and gathered flea-market silver and glassware are perfect to mix on the table. No rules or matching necessary—use what you love.

The Glasses

The stemware is another opportunity to add detail to the story. For some occasions, heavy glasses with a rich color or deep, cut-crystal styles are a good choice.

For a graceful touch, gilded coupes or red wine stems can tie a table of mixed styles together nicely and make it feel more sophisticated. On the other hand, for spur-of-the-moment gatherings, streamlined, clear, restaurant-style glasses or quilted mason jars might be all you need.

Some of my favorite glasses are these delicate etched vintage crystal wineglasses, which I found on a thrift store shelf marked down to just $1.50 each after they had sat for too long unnoticed. They have the most exquisite details on their stems, and the floral etchings on the sides add a beautiful touch that makes you feel a tad fancier while using them.

If using multiple glasses on your table, they don't all need to be the same pattern. They don't even need to be the same combination of patterns from place to place. Choosing your mix is part of the joy of creating a tablescape.

The Flatware

Flatware provides endless possibilities that add another layer to your table. Gold and bold, vintage tarnished or polished silver, modern lines or detailed patterns are flexible. There are many options to fit any occasion.

You can mix and match pieces of silver for a gathered look or go with all matching pieces for more streamlined settings. There is no right or wrong look; it is simply personal choice and what looks good to you for the occasion.

I personally love mismatched vintage silver, and I tend to leave it a bit on the tarnished side for most tables. Vintage silver brings a sense of tradition, history, and charm—and unpolished, it allows the details to stand out just a bit more and make the table feel more casual and inviting. Your elements don't need to be perfect to be enjoyed; sometimes it is the imperfect that makes the most impact on the table.

Shiny gold with modern lines, this flatware is made extra charming with the addition of a burnt-orange velvet ribbon tied around each place setting.

Linens

I am admittedly not the biggest fan of full table linens. There is something about the look and feel of a raw wood tabletop that I am drawn to, and I prefer that rustic backdrop to anything that feels too polished and formal.

That said, I have been known to incorporate a few favorite cloths when planning more refined settings, which might involve yards of velvet draped over the table and puddling on the floor, or a lovely French linen that gives a comfortable elegance to an everyday setting.

I do love a good linen napkin, though, and have stacks of them ironed and ready to use in the armoire. My favorite linens are vintage, gathered from thrift stores, tag sales, and flea markets, and oftentimes these are not even formal napkins. They might be small tea towels that have a delicate edging, or old handkerchiefs with monogrammed details that catch my eye.

I look for linen versus cotton, and dainty crochet and lace details are always on repeat at my tables. Monogrammed linens of all kinds and alphabet letter will find their way home with me whenever I bump into them.

As a rule, I gravitate toward simple whites and deliciously pale, sun-bleached colors that have an easy-to-mix, delightful softness. I also relish faded rich colors, such as muted purples, grays, and blues.

I find that a soft natural linen in a blush or pale gray works well with most any colors and settings, so I collect more of those than anything.

I prefer linens in a neutral color without a pattern to
allow other tabletop elements, such as these lacy plates and
gilded chargers, to take center stage.

The Candles

It doesn't get more brimming with ambience than candles in old candlesticks covered in drippy wax. I have stacks of candles on hand and use them almost daily, all year-round, to bring in that warm ambience and feeling.

From the living room, to the table, to inside little glass jars tucked into pea gravel, to lanterns lining a path to somewhere, candles in various heights and types are a must for my romantic style. To me, taper candles are some of the most magical, with flames dancing high above the table help to illuminate and brighten late-night conversation.

Something to consider when choosing your candles for a table: drippy candles look absolutely inviting and beautiful, but you may want to protect tabletops from wayward wax. A simple bit of wax paper, a jar lid, or even a vintage saucer underneath will help if you are concerned. I am a big drippy candle fanatic: I feel like they speak about the gatherings that have been, the evenings when the candles burned down low while laughter and good memories were being made.

I collect vintage candlesticks to mix on the table, simply focusing on the color or style—brass or wood, for example. I also adore candles in wee mason jars and glass holders in a variety of sizes. Depending on the size you use, you can gather fifty or more in the center of a long table and have plenty of room. The glow and warmth from a smattering of candles in jars marching down the center of the table in place of a formal centerpiece is incredible.

Of course, safety is the most important consideration with candles. Be sure they are never unattended. I like to burn them down just a bit before guests arrive. An even safer option is faux-realistic flickering candles for the same moody effect without any of the worry, especially when in area where it is not advised to have a flame.

For inexpensive candles in abundance, I make a stop at a dollar store or warehouse store and load up on white candles in simple glasses. You can easily mix the sizes to create a beautiful glow on the table.

The Lighting

String lights are like candles to me; they are pure magic for gatherings. I place them in abundance, running zigzags across branches of a tree and above a table for a dinner party or out-under-the-stars gathering. I also add them to the garden areas and string them in tree branches in the distance for a little bit of background twinkle beauty.

Depending on the size of the area, I usually link several strands together, and LED lights are my first choice—mostly because I enjoy them for hours and hours almost daily in the garden areas and don't want to worry about any heat from a traditional light bulb.

Something to consider: if you don't have a power source, battery-operated string lights are a wonderful alternative. I have placed those small battery-powered twinkles inside a firebox on the wood or down the center of a table for a little bit of extra pizzazz.

Twinkle lights are something I use generously.
They provide a warm glow above the table, which creates a
perfect light for the evening.

The Flowers

Flowers are an essential layer on any table or at any gathering. I love them in buckets, French market baskets, jars of all sizes, chunky pottery, and tucked into garlands and on the napkins at place settings. Some of my favorites are a single type of bloom in abundance and in various stages, with petals dropping and covering the tabletop. There is no wrong way to incorporate that natural beauty into your settings.

When choosing flowers for a table or event, I start with what I am drawn to for the color theme. My go-to for most settings is a pale blush or peach, for which Juliet roses are perfect. I also like to layer shades of a single color—like purple, lilac, and lavender—for a monochromatic arrangement. Blush peonies and ranunculus are long-time favorites that are often on repeat over here.

If my favorites are out of season, I look to the garden for inspiration. Stunning foraged bouquets can be made from golden grasses, wild flowers, and a few sage-colored leaves. In more formal flower gardens, you may find profuse possibilities for selecting blooms and greens for a "gathered goodness" arrangement.

For vases, I like the flowers to shine more than the containers. I love the mix of a rustic vessel with the refined beauty of a flower. Old painted buckets, metal bins, gathering baskets, and zinc or galvanized vessels are some of my favorite picks for large arrangements—even well worn. A jar of water is placed inside any that are no longer watertight.

The greenhouse shelves are filled with random utilitarian garden discards that I've found while thrifting. I also favor clear mason jars, silver creamers, and dainty sugar bowls. Delicate floral containers, like a Limoges creamer with the lid removed or an old tureen with painted flowers or chinoiserie pattern, work beautifully as well.

I tend to go overboard on flowers, for even the simplest arrangement adds beauty to a table. Pitchers in white ironstone, silver plate, or brassy golds and clear glass wine bottles with or without the labels can be grouped on a table, each with a single stem or a couple of stems.

SMALL
GATHERINGS

A SNUG BREAKFAST SETTING IN THE
GREENHOUSE, a beach picnic for two, or an
afternoon break in a little patch of wildflowers—small
gatherings are intimate and less formal than those
that involve a guest list and lots of planning. They
are everyday gatherings. Ones that set up in your
backyard or plan impromptu while vacationing. They
are more about creating a cozy ambiance and quiet
conversation or reflection and are often inspired by
the setting or location.

There is something about those smaller gatherings
that brings remembrances of small plates of cookies
and treats on the porch at grandma's house. They may
seem a tad old-fashioned in some ways, especially in
the day of Pinterest-worthy celebrations and everything being planned so perfectly. Yet they are the most
comfortable and relaxing way to absorb the goodness
of the moment, to catch up on the day and take a
break from routine. Whether you can steal fifteen
minutes between projects or a long couple of hours,
these small everyday interludes are nourishment for
the soul. They are perfect times to catch up and connect with friends and family, to relax and recharge, or
to sit quietly and ponder.

They are some of my favorite gatherings, where a few
moments can fill you with so much good energy and
connection, without all the busyness that goes along
with planning a larger party.

NIBBLES
FOR TWO ON
THE DOCK

Summers seem to be filled with trips to the lake, camping, and picnics just waiting to happen. Living just a few hours from one of the most beautiful lakes in California means that road trips and travel come along each summer. Lake Tahoe is an area that holds many memories for me—I grew up staying in a cabin on the lake every year when I was young and going to summer camp and even skiing on occasion during the winter.

Even now, when driving up and over Donner Pass, there is something about that smell in the air. It is like nowhere else I have been and it takes me right back to those childhood days.

Donner Lake is on the way to Tahoe and is much less populated during summer, which makes it an ideal spot for a quick stop for a picnic or even for a getaway on the lake. It is a wonderful place for simple moments. On a recent stay, with just cozy blankets, a picnic basket full of treats, and an armful of fresh peonies and wildflowers, the most idyllic dock on a quiet lake inspired us to pause and enjoy the simple solitude.

A thermos filled with a hot or cold beverage, a few flaky croissants, fresh berries, and cheese were just right for snacking on while watching the sun disappear behind the mountain. As the light changed and moved across the lake, the brilliant colors danced on the water and the cabins on the other side started lighting up one by one—which was altogether quite magical.

After grabbing a few chairs and a small breakfast
table from the house, we carted them to the dock and
set up for an impromptu evening lakeside.

ABOVE: A lemonade or berry-infused drink is a simple fix for a picnic,
and quilted mason jars are easy to carry along.

OPPOSITE: The vase of roses with a little foraged greenery elevates the
romantic ambience.

I added a few blackberries to a personal-size frosted
vegan cake for a touch of seasonal sweetness. We left the
small table and chairs on the dock overnight, and on
the second night used a fresh linen and added flowers
that we were enjoying in the kitchen.

Morning inspiration the next day was just as
spectacular. Setting up by a bridge for a cup of coffee
and the most peaceful sunrise above the lake was
an incredible start to the day.

I often cart a basket of table and picnic elements in my car. I am always looking for that view, backdrop, or place that inspires me to stop and sit for a bit to soak up that beauty. This wonderful dock overlooking the lake was a great place to start one of our mornings.

OVERLEAF: Vintage camping stools fold up and fit easily in the car, but you can also simply pack a blanket. Fill a thermos with coffee, bring a couple of mugs, and head out to find a place that restores you and soak up the beauty.

GREENHOUSE BRUNCH

Inside a warm and charming greenhouse, the abundance of light and fresh air pouring in created an enchanting spot for relishing a couple bites and a quiet talk, tucked away from the rest of the world.

Most of the time, the greenhouse is part getaway and part work space. The shelves are filled with oodles of old galvanized and painted buckets that are just waiting to be filled, as well as buckets of fresh greens and flowers ready to be clipped and processed for bouquets.

There is a place to relax inside, and the center work "island" becomes a table for two with just a quick wipe-down and a couple of odd stools or chairs.

A space like a greenhouse or garden shed converted to a room is a wonderful spot to enjoy outdoor dining, escaping bugs and the weather. I have sat inside this space and listened to the rain on the roof in the evening while relaxing, and with the twinkle of the chandelier and a string of lights just outside the door, it truly feels like a magical escape in the backyard. And it is an unexpectedly inspiring place for setting up a simple quiet lunch or dinner.

A gathering in a shed or greenhouse can be simple: a pot of coffee and platter of scones, cheese and crackers on a breadboard, or a sandwich cut and shared. The garden is just outside the greenhouse, so a bowl of fresh-picked berries is an easy treat to add. A simple bucket of flowers and candles create a bit of cozy on the old farm table. It is a good place to relax for a few minutes and take a break for a bite while enjoying the abundance of blooms on the shelves.

Being filled with fresh flowers in vintage containers makes the greenhouse feel much like a flower market. I tend to keep blooms separate from each other until creating arrangements, so there are buckets of different shades and styles of flowers that mingle quietly.

A new flower to me, butterfly ranunculus (white) has an enchanting wildflower look with the softest of blushing white blooms. It is a long-lasting cut flower and looks wonderful mixed with lilacs and roses alike.

The greenhouse in spring is a lush part of our yard.
Filled with an abundance of flowers, it's a delightful spot for
an impromptu brunch.

Peonies in buckets are a spring thing. There is no such
thing as too many, in my opinion. I bring them to the greenhouse
to clip and remove leaves then arrange them in various-sized
buckets and vases to enjoy throughout the house.

LILAC TABLE

Spring in California is usually bright and sunny, dotted with a few rainy days to nurture the grasses and early blooming flowers and plants. On occasion, though, we get several gloomy days in a row where the sunshine is hiding behind the clouds and it feels like evening has come early. For me, those days inspire!

The sound of the rain has always been something that spurs creativity. It invigorates me, and I oftentimes find myself reaching for my old-fashioned pen and journal. I sit by the open window, jotting notes, ideas, dreams, and visions on the pages while listening to the rain fall outside and breathing in the fresh air.

In early spring, after having hidden indoors during the winter when weather isn't so welcoming, misty spring weather inspires me to wander out and play a bit. Our lilacs bloom early in California and are found abundantly in the wild as well as in the stores. Trimming lilac branches from the tree with great exuberance can be tricky, because taking too many might mean they won't come back as lush next year. So, I clip just an armful and bring larger bunches home from the market to mix in.

Though I have used dainty vases and small holders, one of my favorite containers for lilacs is a large bucket. This vintage galvanized bucket was perfect, allowing the flowers to lean toward the outside and relax.

I often prefer floral arrangements of a single variety.
A large container of lilacs is perfect on its own.

Simplicity on the table continues with small glass jar candles grouped to create a warm glow. Quilted mason jars filled with rosy lemonade are decorated with sprigs of rosemary and lavender for a touch of sweetness.

I tied the vintage flatware with rich eggplant-colored velvet ribbons for an elegant touch before placing them on the plates. Adding a sprig of flowers or herbs to a bundle of flatware and tying the napkin underneath makes a lovely display.

A rustic layered vanilla cake topped with almond frosting sits atop a large slice of bark-covered log that serves as a platter. Rustic platters are the yin to the yang of the elegant cake and create quite a charming look on the table.

Sprigs of lavender and clippings of rosemary and olive branches are wrapped around the base and dotted with fresh blueberries.

Layers of string lights create a warm glow along the with candles and invite guests to sit and enjoy the evening and company just a bit longer. For chilly nights, a chunky basket with freshly laundered blankets set by the table is a welcome comfort for wrapping up around the shoulders and legs and encourages lingering late around the table.

Clipped lilacs from the yard are mixed with flower market lilacs for a large table bouquet. I also spread lilacs in small containers throughout the house in spring; their delicate flowers and scent are enchanting.

OPPOSITE: A sprig of lilac is a lovely addition to the place settings,
simply tied with a velvet ribbon together with the flatware.
Guests can take the sprig home as a memento of the get-together.

ABOVE: Candles and soft, clear lights set the stage for
an enchanting evening.

OPPOSITE: Infused tea is a light drink for spring. Use fresh, organic lavender that has been cleaned as an accent inside the jar.

THIS PAGE: A four-layer vanilla cake with almond frosting is as delicious as it is pretty. It is topped with blueberries, organic fresh roses, and a sprig of olive branch. I often use delicate sugar flowers instead of fresh; they look incredibly real and I don't need to worry about whether the flowers are food-safe.

SWEETS
IN THE
SWEET PEAS

The land our home sits on was one of the first things that drew me to the house and made me feel that our family would be happy here. I wandered the acreage, discovering hidden hollows, grassy meadows, and many fruit trees. At the back of the property, running from one side across to the other, was a very proper-looking line of tall cedar trees planted just so, perfectly spaced.

Having moved into the house in late autumn, much of the landscape was already wearing fall colors or winter branches, so that first spring brought much excitement as each of the plants and trees woke up and started to bloom. And that line of trees in the back did something amazing as well. Underneath each of those trees, what we originally thought to be overgrown weeds turned out to be naturally growing sweet peas. A hillside covered in wild sweet peas looks incredibly beautiful, with their pink, white, and purple blooms mingling amid the vines.

Years later, those sweet peas continue to grow in abundance every spring and summer and always inspire me to capture and share their beauty.

The summer sun starts to drop behind the tips of the trees in late afternoon, providing a warm yet shaded area for lounging in the chaise, taking a siesta in the hammock, or setting up a small table.

This table was an impromptu one that we decided to set in the sweet peas for a family gathering. With the shade of the tall trees above and the carpet of blooms underfoot, it felt like a magical little spot for us to gather for late-afternoon refreshments and lively conversation.

I am a girl who loves symmetry, but I also adore a good mix and mingle. So, for this table, I gathered a few mismatched flea market chairs from my ever-growing collection.

A lightweight bushel basket full of fresh-cut, dainty, daisy-looking wildflowers and ruffled peonies was a simple centerpiece. The flowers were placed inside a plastic bucket set inside the basket, which is a perfect way to use a container that does not actually hold water for a fresh flower arrangement.

Vintage purple stemware and my grandmother's china mingle with a collection of cream-colored embossed vintage plates that are less than perfect, with crazing and a few chips, but that lend a comfortable feeling. I don't shy away from using favorite patterns or pieces simply because they show age. Quite the opposite: I feel they are favorites—the most sought after, as they show they were well loved and used often. Elegant vintage china and pottery are not just pretty pieces that should be kept safe and sound inside the cupboard; I believe they should be enjoyed for everyday occasions as well as special ones.

As the sun started to set behind the trees and the sunlight danced across the sweet peas, we lit the candles and settled in for an early evening chat.

This simple setting in our backyard shows that sometimes a most inspiring spot for a gathering with friends and family doesn't have to be traveled to. Sometimes the perfect place is just outside your own door.

OPPOSITE: Drippy candles and brass candlesticks are some of my favorite things. These are regular candles that started to drip a bit when a light breeze kicked up, and the result was this abundance of charm. I leave the wax on the candlesticks and let the next candle color layer over the previous. It reminds me of gatherings past and how, on the most blissful nights, the candles burn down low.

ABOVE: Vintage china and blush linen napkins are exquisite with purple stemware, while the peonies covering the table with petals show that flowers provide layers of beauty during their stages of life.

WINE COUNTRY BRUNCH FOR TWO

When we first pulled into the driveway of a winery in the central coast one early evening, we were mesmerized by the 1800s farmhouse, white barn, and an enormous oak tree perched on top of a vineyard-covered hill.

It was almost as if that towering tree was watching over the land, set high above anything else, surrounded by the rolling vineyards and providing a lovely bit of shade for quiet moments.

That tree instantly inspired setting up a vintage bench to enjoy a small bite to eat and a refreshing glass of wine on while watching the sunset. We carried a small vintage cane bench with dainty lines and details up the hill and placed it near the base of the tree in the shade of its branches. For a low table, we simply tipped over half a wine barrel to create a table top. Half wine barrels are often reserved for holding trees or vining plants, and you can find them at home improvement stores as well as your local winery. Though barrel ends aren't always perfectly flat on the bottom, even with their wonky, uneven boards, they can readily hold a vintage silver tray of seasonal cheeses, fresh fruits, and crisp crackers.

To supplement a bouquet of seasonal flowers—peonies, roses, and Queen Anne's lace—I clipped a few vines of lush grape leaves with tiny grapes right off the grapevine to tuck inside.

Setting a table for two can be done nearly
anywhere, including on top of a full or halved oak wine barrel.

I brought a silver platter full of Brie, Tuscan cheese, crackers, and fruits to be enjoyed with rosé and a side of the incredible winery view.

My husband carried the cane settee and a half wine barrel
found on the property up to the 300-year-old oak tree.
It was a magnificent spot to savor the sunset.

FLOWER-LADEN TÊTE-À-TÊTE

You don't have to travel far and wide to find a perfect spot for an intimate gathering. The ideal place might be just outside your front door. This towering old camellia tree in our front yard is absolutely covered in the most beautiful flowers every spring. As the blooms fade and new ones open up, the old heads drop to the ground and carpet the lawn with incredible pink petals.

It is a romantic spot for setting a table or even just plopping a couple of pillows to sit on and soak up the beauty.

The lush blooms of this camellia tree in our front yard every winter and spring make a fairy-tale backdrop for a private conversation.

ABOVE: A small crate and cups of tea are enough. It doesn't have
to be a full table to enjoy an inspired setting. Think small, stolen moments
in the middle of the day.

OPPOSITE: Dropped blossoms on an outdoor table take the place of a
cloth for a romantic candlelit supper.

WINE &
CHEESE ON
THE PATIO

I am a huge fan of casual get-togethers—the ones that are all about good food, good company, and lots of laughter, without any formal setup or fuss.

In California, we spend much of our time outside and consider the outdoor areas to be an extension of our indoor spaces. Outdoor living truly is what we do.

For simple get-togethers with a few friends, there is nothing easier than putting together a beautiful cheese board and wine pairing. I start with an oversized vintage breadboard; these can be found at flea markets and online vintage sources. I layer cheeses, fruits, breadsticks, crackers, fresh jam, nuts, and chunks of semisweet chocolate for a bit of sweetness.

Being vegetarian, I do not include traditional charcuterie on my boards, but, of course, you can add whatever your favorites are.

Our lion fountain patio is a favorite spot to gather
for a fruit and cheese board in the spring.

With the Cecile Brunner roses climbing over the fence
and intertwining with the ivy, the patio feels full of
spring even on an overcast evening.
The tree stump is an impromptu table for an oversize
vintage breadboard hosting layers of nibbles.

Creating the Cheese Board

For this cheese board, we started with fruits.

Fruits—Red grapes, fresh-picked blackberries, blueberries, and apple slices.

Cheeses—A small round of Brie, a Tuscan wedge, Cranberry Stilton, and a goat cheese log are perfect and offer a variety of sweet and savory flavors.

Nuts—Peppered and salted cashews and pistachios are a delightful addition. I also favor raw almonds and Marcona almonds.

Accompaniments—A bowl of Mediterranean olives and feta provides nibbles, and dried Turkish figs will do the trick in place of fresh.

Breads—I generally include breads or crackers and a fresh sweet jam for topping.

Sweets—For a touch of sweetness, chunks of semisweet or very dark chocolate make guests feel like they have had a full course.

ENTERTAINING AT HOME

OUR HOME IS ALWAYS OPEN TO FRIENDS and family who stop by. Hosting guests for an afternoon or a few days is one of my favorite things. We are a little bit out of the way, so occasionally, staying over is a good way to extend a visit. Much of my entertaining is casual, and sometimes those simple chats over morning coffee and breakfast or conversations by the fire or fountain at night with friends are exactly what I need to rejuvenate my soul.

Over the years, we have hosted many of those simple gatherings, as well as the traditional birthday parties, graduation parties, and even last-minute ladies' nights on occasion. I love when the house is full, when there is that bustle in the room, and I relish creating moments, tables, and gatherings that make my guests feel doted on.

Of course, an impromptu guest knocking on the door can send any host into a bit of a flurry when it comes to food. Something I have learned is to have a few staples on hand all the time—pasta, marinara sauce, a plentiful supply of fresh veggies at the market each week, for example. And if a market is not far, a loaf of fresh-baked French bread can become a delicious bruschetta or garlic bread in just a few minutes.

Since I usually have fresh flowers in the house—it is one of my weekly treats—I can readily break up a larger bouquet into several jar-sized bouquets to create a beautiful centerpiece in minutes and also move some smaller ones to fill the house with a warmth from room to room. Another tip is to have plenty of candles in various sizes available to light as needed. The flicker of candles adds a lovely ambience for dinners and evening gatherings.

UNDER
THE
OAK TREE

One of our favorite trees is a towering oak that sits in the front of the house. Someone long ago built a concrete patio next to the tree and added an incredible rock fireplace at one side. It is a sunny, warm area all year long, and in summer it can become unbearably hot until the sun drops behind the trees. But the evenings are absolutely incredible—warm enough to be comfortable without wrapping up in a sweater and cool enough to enjoy a small fire next to the table for ambience.

A table that is almost too heavy to move sits at the center of the patio under the tree. Its silvery, reclaimed-oak top becomes part of the rustic table setting. A simple linen runner is a foundation for several clear wine bottles that hold white and barely blushing peonies and fresh-clipped Cecile Brunner climbing roses.

Clear wine or water bottles, with or without charming labels, are lovely layered on the table in threes or fives for holding a few stems of flowers each. A tip is to offset the bottle vases from the place settings just a bit so guests can see each other and reach across to share plates of appetizers. I also like to add smaller pitchers and extra cups filled with flowers to add lower layers of blooms as well.

As often happens while dining outdoors, the warmth of the weather and a breeze bring about somewhat droopy layers of petals in the blooms that, as they fall, some would say cause a bit of a mess. To me, it is a beautiful mess, and I tend to leave those fallen petals and use them to my advantage for the settings.

For casual nibbles under the oak, I chose a small, personal-sized bread board topped with various cheeses, crackers, small cups of berries and jams, and larger vintage platters of things like croissants, crusty breads, and desserts.

OPPOSITE: An old farmhouse table set under a towering oak tree is a
charming spot for an everyday occasion. This table was moved onto the
patio and the string lights were added to the branches in late spring,
before the gathering started. A few things to consider when
setting up in a new spot: How far it is to power for your electric lights?
What type of flooring base do you have to work with?
This poured-concrete patio creates a more stable setup than areas
with a dirt floor or foliage.

ABOVE: Wine bottles with beautiful labels and mason jars in several sizes,
each holding ruffly peonies, take the place of a large centerpiece.
Various heights and limiting each arrangement to just a few flowers allow
easy across-the-table conversation without forgoing beauty.

A beautiful mess—scattered blooms and petals, candles, delicious cheeses, warm coffee, delicate china, silver plate flatware, and blush glasses. An imperfectly perfect view for a lovely get-together.

A variety of foods on the table is always appreciated.
Guests can grab what they like and leave what they don't
for someone else to enjoy. Croissants, Brie, rustic bread,
and scones suit my French country style.

A TABLE IN
THE WOODS

Autumn is a season of abundance, filled with colors and ambience as nature puts on a brilliant display. It is also harvest time for apples and grapes. The crisp mornings and evenings are perfect for wandering in the woods, with leaves covering paths and crunching underfoot. There is a heavy scent that signals "cozy" and inspires me to gather, create, and delight with a table set among all that beauty.

We have acres and acres of forested land not far from our home and some on our own property. Back behind a line of trees that divides the open and wooded areas, there is a little path that meanders along. Tucked into tall grasses and wild blackberry bushes, it is an enchanted little walk that leads to an old hollow tree that we call the "raccoon tree," as we found a family of raccoons nesting among the branches one year. That dirt path is dotted with old apple, cedar, and pine trees and is also filled with sweet pea blooms underfoot every spring. In fall, those sweet peas turn to a shade of brown as the chill sets in—and it was that moody feeling that appeared with the season that inspired me to set a table under the apple tree branches.

Setting a table that is not near the house requires a bit more carting of this and that to get the area ready for guests. But I have found that something as simple as a large French market basket is ideal for carrying various things like candles, napkins, and flatware to the site. After a few trips up and down the path with various tabletop elements, flowers, and food, it is time to turn on the twinkle lights and enjoy the warm autumn mood.

Gathering some fallen pine cones and acorns from the forest floor is a wonderful way to tie the table decoration to the environment.

I think any table in the woods will be one that is inspired—whether it is draped with a tartan throw for an informal picnic or covered with elegant florals for a fancy wedding celebration. But when it comes to just a small bit of decadence and refined elegance, those dainty details are perfection—like mix and match gilded glasses and delicate lace plates.

The stemware is mixed—vintage etched-crystal goblets that are some of my favorites are well paired with little gilded coupes. I am not a stickler for certain sizes and styles of glasses being used for exact purposes, and you will often find my tables with "like" goblets and flatware rather than exactly the same at each setting. The coupes are nice for sipping something delicious, as well as for serving a bit of caramel-drizzled ice cream or cobbler to be eaten with a dainty spoon.

Creamy velvet napkins add the perfect touch of luxe, and gathered seasonal fruit creates a charming centerpiece.

The flowers for this table were inspired by the rustic setting and the silver trophy vessel. Though I love pink peonies and ranunculus, when it comes to roses, my choice is almost always white and barely blushing shades. I love that rosy whites can be dressed up or down and can be equally beautiful either way. These are $6 everyday white roses from the market, mixed with very pale blush garden roses from a local farmer. A few sprigs of eucalyptus and various seasonal greens are mixed with grasses and rich red leaves for a bit of drama, with the fun addition of golden yellow billy buttons, genus Craspedia. Sometimes just a touch of that golden color is all it takes to warm up an arrangement and give it an autumnal feeling.

In the background view, the barn is dotted with pumpkins on the porch and path, while a crystal-laden chandelier twinkles away inside, inviting guests to wander down the path to the long table in the barn for prolonged conversations.

Glitzy gold flatware is a choice I favor all year long. Bundling
each place setting with velvet ribbon is a luxurious touch.
I often find inexpensive yardage of vintage ribbon at thrift
stores and collect it for later opportunities.

Detailed vintage stemware and brass candlesticks are collected from thrift shopping over the years. I use them over and over, in many stylings—which shows that if you love something, you will bring it out to enjoy often.

BELOW, LEFT: Treasured delicate china and gilded coupes set
the stage for a beautiful table.

BELOW, RIGHT: A collection of vintage and reproduction glassware
is as pretty in waiting as it is on the table.

OPPOSITE: A small cake stacked with lemon and buttercream
and topped with fresh fruit sits on a wood slice. A cake idea: Buy a unique
special-order bakery cake and then embellish it for your occasion.
This one was a rectangular cake that I sliced into two sections
and stacked; then I added fresh blueberries, sliced figs, and sprigs of
rosemary, which gave it a whole new vibe.

The flowers are a mix of gathered and market finds. The larger
bouquet, which spreads across the corner of the table
(and creates a "moment" outside the barn), includes garden grasses
and fresh greens; I let the longer ones fan out to the sides. The roses
are a mix of garden spray roses and garden roses, and for an unexpected
pop, yellow Craspedia (aka billy buttons).

CHIC BARN CELEBRATION

When the darkness and chill of the night start to settle in, if you follow the dirt path through the trees, it leads to a small barn, where the evening continues. The cozy space is perfect for hosting a larger dinner and staying late to enjoy a glass of wine and conversation that lingers into the night.

Inside the doors, a crystal-covered chandelier lights the barn and illuminates it with a sprinkling of magic. I am a big believer in chandeliers in any setting, and a barn is no different. The beautiful crystals are a perfect foil to the simple whitewashed walls with exposed framing.

Beneath the chandelier, an antique drapery table wears the most delightful chippy remnants of its original soft pistachio colored paint. The mostly bare-wood finish forgives any spills or messes. The table is surrounded by antique French chairs wearing simple burlap and linen on the front. Though the fabric is worn and faded and the chairs seem to be in the middle of restoration—the mingle is perfect to me. Their well-loved patina and character tell a story and their faded glamour steals the show.

For this setting, I designed a simple centerpiece of candles, fresh fruit, and dried fruit potpourri scattered down the center of the table. I love using fruit and vegetables in my summer and autumn stylings when they are in abundance. They add so much visual beauty to the table and sometimes can be snacked on throughout the evening if someone is so inclined. The fresh potpourri also adds a sweet autumn scent that fills the air.

The place settings here were kept simple. Dishes that are quietly beautiful in a handmade modern and slightly irregular shape wear the softest blush color sprinkled with brown speckles. They are perfect for enjoying a slice of flower-topped cake, a sliver of cantaloupe, or few bites from the cheese platter. The etched glasses are some of my favorites; I found a set of them tucked onto a shelf behind glass at the thrift store for around a dollar a piece.

They are repeated on my tables often, as they mix with elegant expensive stemware and every-day stemware just as easily as they make a statement on their own.

At the end of the room is a large antique trumeau mirror with a beautifully carved frame and soft pale green paint leaning against the wall. The looking glass is more mottled than perfect, but, even so, it reflects the candle and chandelier light beautifully across the room.

Behind the table, an antique marble replace mantel salvaged from a Victorian home makes a place for changing vignettes such as artwork, flowers, candles, and seasonal decorations.

The stage for a gathering starts before guests reach
the appointed spot for dining. Here, a fresh greens garland
and candles welcome guests coming up the path.

OPPOSITE: I always let the cake take its place on the table as a star
in the décor before it is sliced and devoured.

ABOVE: Blush garden roses, mini spray garden roses, and antique-color
hydrangeas mix with lisianthus and a few eucalyptus stems.

ABOVE: A scattering of potpourri and fresh fruits, like peaches and
Bosc pears, creates a natural and aromatic centerpiece.

OPPOSITE: A vintage crock from Italy holds a mixed bouquet.
The garden roses, spray roses, hydrangeas, Craspedia, and eucalyptus
echo the flowers on a table along the pathway to the barn and tie the
two settings together for the evening.

Antique chairs backed in a luxurious original chenille fabric add an elegant touch that balances their burlap-covered fronts. The well-loved table is an antique drapery table from France. It wears lovely bits of its original pistachio green paint that has chipped and worn away over the years.

Elegant-Rustic Layer Cake

Cakes topped with fruit and flowers have become one of my signature party
desserts, and I have several ways of creating them.

If time is not of the essence, I will bake cake rounds for the creation that I have in mind.
But if it is a bit of rush, I will call a local bakery and order the cake
rounds and a container of fresh frosting that I can customize, and then I create the layers
and details at home. This is a simple and quick way to get a cake in as many layers as you
would like and in any custom combination.

This cake has three layers of chocolate with a custom creamy almond buttercream in
between. These are topped with a stack of three smaller layers of white cake. I frosted the
outside of both sections and then used a baker's offset spatula to remove much of the
frosting, leaving it with a rustic look.

After the frosting was just right, I added a few elegant garden-grown flowers. For a touch
of greens, I love to use herbs. This cake has a few clippings of lemon thyme tucked into
the flowers and a few sprigs on the platter.

IMPORTANT NOTE ABOUT USING FRESH FLOWERS WITH FOOD:

It is imperative that you make sure the flowers you use are safe to be used with food,
are free of any pesticides and sprays, and are washed and clean. You can consult
your bakery for advice on flower varieties that are safe, and they can oftentimes
recommend the florist or gardener they use for sourcing organic flowers.

As an added precaution, I always use a barrier in between to keep the flowers from
touching the cake. These are available at your bakery as well.

You can also use incredibly realistic sugar creations for a similar look to a real flower.

Think outside the box when looking for a serving platter
for your cakes and other baked goods.
The one shown here is a vintage floral platter that dresses
the table and adds to the overall décor.

DINING ROOM
CASUAL
LUNCH

The dining room is often reserved for formal occasions—those dinners that have tables set with the finest china in the cupboard, expensive glasses, and polished silver. But I am of the thought that the dining room should be enjoyed for everyday occasions as much as formal ones.

Our dining area lacks the formality of a room with four walls. Since our dining area is in part of the living room, it is a place for meals with lively conversations every day, all year long. It is easy to pull up a chair and enjoy a quick sandwich while visiting with someone who might be relaxing on the sofa.

On the table is an easy, elegant setting. The simple blush dishes are everyday favorites for a no-fuss table. Elegant glassware and vintage collected silver flatware are mixed at the place settings and add a touch of formality to the otherwise simple setting.

Antique Italian pottery is filled with fresh market blooms and gathered garden elements: white and blush roses, alstroemeria, eucalyptus, and dahlias create elegant yet casual arrangements. Another smaller bouquet tucked onto a shelf in the cupboard echoes their look.

ABOVE: Simple blush dishes and mixed vintage silver flatware are pieces
I use frequently. And fresh figs add another charming—and edible—
element to the center of the table.

OPPOSITE: Pretty linen slipcovers dress up our dining chairs while
protecting them from crumbs and spills.

OPPOSITE: An antique armoire stands tall behind the table with doors
open to reveal the shelves. Brass goblets, stacks of plates,
and an old silver dome mingle with pottery, books, and architectural
elements. Shelves are an opportunity to create a "moment" and add more
interest for your diners. A bouquet or dried floral crown on top of dishes
will spark comments and help people feel at ease.

HARVEST TABLE

When there is a chill in the air and the leaves begin to change color and the grapevines are heavy with fruit, it is a harvest party season—a time for friends and family to gather to celebrate the season's bounty, harvest the grapes, and enjoy a dinner together out under the harvest moon.

This time of year in the wine country is like no other. It is a busy time of gathering fruit, with vineyards dotted in leaves that turn from vibrant green to gold and amber. They are full of rich, dark grapes ready to be picked. The charm of those rolling vineyards inspires everyday entertaining out on the porch or at a table nestled near the vines to soak up all that ambience.

A rustic table brought out from the barn finds a perfect spot under an oak tree right next to the heart of the vineyard at my brother's Calistoga home. Chippy green bistro chairs, everyday white dishes, and a mixed collection of vintage crystal glasses have an eclectic gathered feeling.

For the table décor, look no further than the grapevines for clippings of greens and grapes to lay down the center with squatty peaches, figs, and olives, which are all in abundance this time of year. They are perfect for nibbling on as well as for creating an organic and natural centerpiece. Oftentimes the best table elements are right outside, and you don't have to look beyond your backyard to find the perfect mix of seasonal touches.

The best part of a harvest dinner is that it truly embodies the feeling of season by using the farm-to-table approach of fruits from the vineyards, local orchards, and organic gardens in a mishmash of this and that. The fun is that no formal menu need be planned in advance; it can be based on the day's gatherings at the market, bringing edibles like fresh greens, crusty breads, marinated olives, and delicious fruit desserts for an inspired seasonal meal.

An antique farm table that was used for sorting grapes is repurposed for everyday dinners. We gathered metal bistro chairs around it and set the table by the vineyard for a harvest party held for family and neighbors.

ABOVE: Vintage cut crystal glasses in mixed patterns march
down the table. Don't be afraid to combine stemware; not every table
needs perfectly matched place settings.

OPPOSITE: Drippy candles and fruit from the fall harvest
are an artful centerpiece.

OPPOSITE: I always love to capture a "moment" while hosting a gathering. An old chair set in the middle of the vineyard is perfect for placing our bouquet. Always-elegant white roses, blush stocks, and eucalyptus are accented by some of the vineyard clippings.

ABOVE: Wee brioche is wrapped in baker's paper and tied with twine. A sprig of rosemary is tucked in for eye appeal.

ABOVE: These are wine grapes, which are on the tart side for snacking, but my nieces, Elodie and Willa, showed us where the Concord grapes are and made sure that we clipped some of those as well.

OPPOSITE: We brought a favorite bike along with us for a few rides in the wine country and, of course, to enjoy picking a couple bunches of the grapes and cart them back in a crate.

A GRAZING BREAKFAST IN THE KITCHEN

Sometimes the best gathering tables are the ones that aren't planned to perfection. The ones that are made up of gathered market bounty from the morning shopping: fresh local seasonal fruits and vegetables, simple grains, and stacks of warm waffles with melted butter. A grab-what-speaks-to-you kind of meal. One that focuses more on the conversation over coffee than the details of the china—though that is beautiful too.

I love a grazing table for several reasons, the first being that it is so easy to put together. A grazing table is made up of anything and everything you would like it to be, and it is an informal and casual way to serve up a wonderful meal with friends and family.

This breakfast was impromptu, perfect for a few late-night guests who stayed over at the last minute. It is an ideal way to quickly host out-of-town family who drop in unexpectedly. A grazing table can also be a labor-saving alternative for special occasions such as Thanksgiving or Christmas, when most of you want to save your energy for the "big" event of the day.

For this grab-and-go breakfast, the choices are jars are filled with oats topped with fresh berries, layers of fresh fruit for the taking, yogurt with granola, sliced grapefruit topped with chunky sugar or warmed honey, stacks of buttermilk waffles, breakfast breads, croissants, and muffins. If you want to add meat options, the possibilities for enjoying breakfast are endless.

PREVIOUS OVERLEAF: A different day, a different breakfast view—this time with lemon cakes, lemon and blueberry waffles, and fresh-squeezed lemon water for a refreshing start to the day. When creating a grazing breakfast, simply layer fruits, breads, muffins, and anything else you would like to include and add little jars of preserves, maple syrup, and butter. Add a pot of French press coffee, hot water, and other elements and let guests serve themselves.

OPPOSITE: An assortment of delicious options gathered on the island in the kitchen shows your guests how happy you are that they came. Stacks of warm waffles with toppings of berries and peaches are a crowd pleaser.

BELOW: Easy oats in a jar with fruit is a favorite to make, and vintage cups somehow make the coffee and tea more delicious.

BACKYARD GLAMPING

A little imagination turned this normally grassy area from a nothing spot into a fabulous place to entertain friends for the evening. With string lights dangling from the branches and dozens of candles as a centerpiece, the decoration of the makeshift table created a feeling somewhere between camping out and a bohemian get-together under the stars.

A long pallet used for holding firewood in winter became a workable table placed on the ground, with wide-plank reclaimed boards added to the top, and a dozen pillows on either side enticed guests to plop down and get cozy.

No fancy floral arrangement or formal bouquets for this table. The centerpiece is all about ambience—candles of various sizes in glass containers do the talking. These are easy to find at dollar shops in sets of two or four; for very little investment, you have a centerpiece full of charm. For safety's sake, don't leave them unattended, of course, but another favorite trick is to use realistic faux candles in place of, or in addition to, real ones.

The bouquets were gathered from the wildflower garden by the greenhouse. Cosmos, lamb's ear, sage, and lavender, along with butterfly bush and any other seasonal blooms I could find, were placed into large mason jars and tucked among the candles.

Across the way, the copper fire-pit lounge area was ideal for warming hands or relaxing during the evening. I prefer a seating group of individual chairs, which always makes people feel more relaxed and at home. Late evenings often involve nibbles like a pot of melted Brie with various toppings to enjoy with crusty bread and a glass of wine.

A summer get-together inspired this low, bohemian-style gathering. A table was created by laying pallets for a base and adding several reclaimed boards to create a level top. Next, stacks of pillows to lounge on. Then it was all about adding that tabletop ambience with focus on the candles, blooms, and vintage drinkware.

Combined light from the bulbs, twinkles, and fire pit gave
this evening a magical feeling.

Whether the cheese is melted on the stove or at the fire pit, the feeling of a fondue party outdoors is really something special.

Campfire Brie

In a cast-iron skillet or another low, wide pan, place a small wheel
of Brie inside and heat it over the open flames of your fire pit
or on the kitchen range.

Once it's melted, add your toppings and provide fondue forks for dipping
chunks of crusty bread into the delectable melted cheese or a larger
utensil for serving scoops onto individual plates.

A FEW POSSIBLE TOPPINGS:

· Sliced tomatoes and basil

· Roasted garlic

· Sun-dried tomatoes

· Fruits or jams (apricot, blackberry, and fig are delicious)

· Caramelized nuts

151

INSPIRATIONAL
SETTINGS

TAKING A FEW MINUTES TO WATCH THE SUN rise over the lake from a mountaintop road, an old dock on a quiet lake, a field dotted with wildflowers in the spring, or tall wheat blowing in the autumn breeze is truly an indulgent pleasure.

When traveling, I tend to stop and soak up moments quite often. Recognizing this inclination, I usually have a favorite blanket, pillows, and a basketful of impromptu picnic goodies in my car.

When I find a location that inspires a more organized gathering, I send an invite to friends to save the date and then start planning the logistics: the table and chairs, the food, the flowers, the ambience.

Of course, some locations are harder than others. Setting up an evening on a dock across the street from a lake cabin where you are staying is a fairly easy setup for carting a small table and chairs, while staging in an apple orchard or a field might be a little harder due to accessibility by vehicle and the distance you need walk and transport your things. In the second case, good organizing will make all the difference, and an inspiring setting can create the most incredible gatherings and memories.

Think outside the box. For a special gathering with friends over a bite of dessert in the apple orchard, I pulled out a $15 thrift store chair and placed it in the flowers. This charming little moment was a spot for guests to take photos.

FLOWER MEADOW PICNIC

A jaunt through California fields in the spring found us meandering into a beautiful state park. Its well-traveled roads wound along an area known for its glorious display of wildflowers, with majestic flower-covered mountains on both sides.

Park rangers and maps showed the locations where people are allowed to picnic, take photos, and hike into the fields and mountains; the trails, almost hidden by wildflowers, led to even more paths less traveled and expanses of quiet beauty. We stayed on the clearly marked paths as we hiked so as not to disrupt the wild growth.

We found a lovely spot next to a lookout area with views of yellow and purple wildflowers as far as the eye could see, and we settled into one of the many clearings that were available to soak up that beauty while enjoying a sweet treat. Lemon iced tea and a fresh fruit pie picked up on the way are wonderful pick-me-up snacks for a midday picnic. A wooden crate flipped over made a suitable table, or the top of a picnic basket could work just as well.

I often have picnic and table bits packed in my car—
cloths, pillows, and a basket holding clean cutlery and
dishes. When we happen upon something that
makes us stop the car, we take the luxury of sitting for a
bit to soak up the inspiration.

APPLE ORCHARD PIE SOCIAL

Over the river and through the woods, as they say. A small, winding road in the countryside can sometimes lead to the most unexpected opportunities for an inspired table. On this particular trip, a beautiful apple orchard on rolling hills made us pull the car over for a closer look. The owner of the orchard is a farmer who also has a restaurant and fruit stand on the property, and after chatting with the owner, we planned and set up a table in a middle of an apple orchard.

Rows and rows of apple trees marched down both sides of a grassy lane just so—their branches peppered with colorful apples in the richest tones of rosy reds and blush pinks—and repeated over rolling hillsides as far as the eye could see. Older orchards such as this one have a sense of history and charm, and I loved wandering through the orchard rows with a bucket in hand, picking a few apples to snack on.

An evening with friends to enjoy a seasonal dessert can be as simple or decadent as you would like. You can grab a favorite blanket and some personal-size pies for your guests to nibble on while watching the birds flit from one tree to the next. Or you can set up a table, as we did for this gathering. We moved a slightly wonky farmhouse table with chunky legs and a worn tabletop into an open spot between areas of the trees, and we purchased several of the restaurant's fresh-made berry pies in various sizes and flavors for sharing with friends. Such a simple way to enjoy a warm afternoon or evening in a beautiful setting.

For this gathering, we went to the place where apple pies begin and set up a table amid rows of apple trees still wearing the season's glory.

OPPOSITE: In any setting, a chair, stool, small table, crate, or basket can provide an opportunity for a sprinkle of magic. This chair invites guests to snap a few fun photos for remembering the occasion.

BELOW: Fresh mini blackberry pies are just right for single servings or bite-size slices. Sprigs of confirmed edible organic flowers or sugar flowers add whimsy.

A bucketful of apples sits on a chair at sunset.
Sometimes enchantment comes from the simplest of
things seen in a different light.

ABOVE: The bouquet is a congenial mingling of roses,
Cafe au Lait dahlias, maroon dahlias, and yarrow
dotted with fresh eucalyptus.

OPPOSITE: The juxtaposition of rustic elements with refined china
plates is one of my favorite looks for outdoor tables.

VINEYARD FORMAL DINNER

I have long had a fascination with old barns. I remember driving through the countryside in the Midwest and noticing the weathered barns that appeared around every corner. Barns are utilitarian, for the most part, providing shelter and warmth for farm animals and a place to keep hay storage dry; but they also have a huge amount of character that naturally draws the eye.

At a beautiful vineyard on the Central Coast of California, I knew right away that this barn was the perfect location for a special-occasion dinner. Tall and stately, its enormous doors opened wide in the front to a pea gravel area beneath a rolling hill covered in vines, with a stately oak standing watch.

For the event, I left the oversize tables bare to gather up the warmth from the wood as part of the overall rustic setting. The place settings were comprised of some of my favorite lace-detailed plates, wine stems, and vintage wood-and-gold flatware. Blush linen napkins added a touch of rosy warmth, while flickering candles provided a soft glow for quiet conversations.

The flower bouquets set in mason jars were paced down the table. They were a mix of flower market goodness that had caught my eye; hellebores, peonies, garden roses, eucalyptus, and dahlias all created a warm, late-summer feeling on the table.

Dining al fresco while protected from the hot sun
is the best of both worlds. The view of this California
vineyard in summer is quite glorious.

171

For a formal evening dinner, the barn provides another
sublime view along with cross-ventilation. Three bouquets
are strategically placed so as to not block the view of people
sitting directly across the table from each other.

Flower bouquets marching down the table are sumptuous and yet casual in mason jars. A mix of hellebores, peonies, garden roses, eucalyptus, and dahlias carry the color theme of the evening.

OPPOSITE: Wine barrels and a few stools are a perfect place for guests to mingle before dinner is served.

ABOVE: It is all in the mix. The detailed plates indicate a more formal event, while the natural elements tone down the fanciness and make a more comfortable table setting. A custom bakery creation, this is a formal iced cake that was topped with fresh blackberries and sprigs of rosemary as a garnish.

Pretty bouquets are posed for their obligatory photo op before
making their way to the dining table.

ABOVE: My favorite lace-detailed plates and amber wine stems look
magical in the glow of candlelight.

OPPOSITE: The side of the barn had a set of two pairs of smaller barn
doors that opened up to reveal a most incredible rolling vineyard view and
a three-hundred-year-old oak tree standing sentinel.

PRIVATE
BEACH PARTY

Salty sea air, warm sand, and incredible sunsets—the ocean is always inspiring to me. It is a first-choice escape for a few hours or a few days, and wrapping up in a blanket to linger while the sun sets is a favorite thing.

Most beach gatherings are informal and rely on the basics—a soft blanket, big pillows, an umbrella, and maybe a couple of chairs, with a basketful of picnic food to enjoy while relaxing. But on occasion, setting up a simple dinner for a couple of friends is a fun thing to do, and it can be as easy as a little extra planning for a low table and a bonfire or making it a tailgate gathering.

Some of our favorite beaches in California allow vehicles right out on the sand or up to the edge, making planning a table that much easier. This brunch at the beach was full of simple pleasures, and it started with a pallet turned into a table. Anything wood with weathered patina speaks to me, and when we came upon stacks of old pallets heading to the recycle, it was a perfect opportunity to grab a couple. Since pallets vary so much in size, we chose a small square one for the beach and simply added chunky old wood legs to give it a bit of height.

Blue glassware and plates echo the color of the water and sky, while the flowers are warm rosy blush and cream tones. No formal settings here—just the basics for sharing a picnic-style meal full of fruit, coffee cake, and lemon water.

This would be just as easy to set up at a beach picnic table, on a blanket, or by a fire pit, if fires are allowed at the beach. Wherever and however you set up, the key is to soak up the inspiration from the beautiful surroundings—relax and enjoy.

A vintage style beach umbrella and pair of sling chairs creates a perfect spot to listen to the waves and relax at water's edge.

A vessel of garden flowers changes the look of the table from utilitarian to grand. Yes, it can be a bit of trouble to carry a vessel with water to the site if it is a far walk—you will probably get wet. But you can also fill the container with bottled water once you get there. Fresh flowers help to make the table uniquely yours.

ABOVE LEFT: Our dog, Sweet Pea, enjoys our outings at the beach. We take
her along whenever it is practical to do so.

ABOVE RIGHT: A stop at a nearby bakery produced the basic substance
of our beach snack this day. Small-town bakeries
are some of the best I've found.

OPPOSITE: Blue and white is a classic look, regardless of the vintage or
specific pattern. It really elevated this ambience of our beach table.

SUMMER FIELDS GATHERING

When the grasses turn from green to gold and grow tall and dance in the breeze, there is just something about those fields full of warm golden tones that entice.

In California, after a rainy spring that brought hearty growth in the fields and farms, those grasses turned a beautiful wheat color in the summer and fall. We came upon this field while on the road one day. It was dotted with towering pines and had mountain views in the distance. The grassy fields were part of a public walking area, which made it a perfect place for an elegant dinner.

We brought a farm table here one evening to gather friends for an autumn dinner. I mixed vintage and farm chairs with different finishes, styles, and natural colors, not caring whether there was a match in the bunch.

A tip on table options: we have used folding sawhorses with planks under cloths, and transported farm tables with legs removed. It does require some planning ahead, but the reward is an evening filled with enchantment.

A beautiful crochet lace cloth signaled a bit more formal feeling while allowing the patina of the tabletop to show through, which prevented it from feeling too refined.

My favorite etched crystal glasses were dollar finds from the thrift store, and washed linen and velvet napkins added a luxurious touch.

Florals were in-season blooms in shades of whites, blushes, and rich maroons.

Lace may seem a bit over the top for a setting in a dry summer field, but contrasting effects well executed are sure to make the occasion memorable.

ABOVE: An armful of fresh market flowers were arranged into a big and beautiful bouquet for our table. I chose flowers in warm colors and tones to complement the palette. Nature provided a beautiful backdrop of rich golden yellows, deep greens, and dusty blues.

OPPOSITE: Flowers nestled on a vintage chair in a lovely outdoor setting. This juxtaposition never gets old.

AUTUMN INTERLUDE

Paths along a creek or through the woods are favorite places to walk and wander; they inspire quiet moments and reflection. In summer, such footpaths are full of rich, vibrant leaves and seem concealed by the green canopies above. Then in autumn, the crisp air changes the colors to rich gold and red tones, and a moody feeling ensues when paths become scattered with fallen leaves and a musty scent rises from the earth after a little rain.

All of those things inspired me to set a few tables that embraced all that rich autumn feeling and set them among the trees. The leaf-covered ground and flowers and foliage gathered nearby helped to create an ambience that was hard to resist.

A rich velvet tablecloth that draped down to the crisp leaves lent a formal feeling, and a bare table in a rich dark wood both contributed to an inspired table that gathered up the warmth and goodness of the season.

Vintage dishes in mismatched patterns, cut-crystal glasses, and vintage silver made a quiet table. Gathered ferns and branches of oak leaves mingled with market flowers in a silver pitcher for a splendid centerpiece.

The velvet cloth is a simple yet elegant addition.
Leaving it unpressed gives it both a formal and casual
look at the same time. Elegance and casualness are
truly proper companions when it comes to setting
a table for a gathering.

OPPOSITE: In the more rustic and gathered table setting, cranberry glass mugs contrast with the flowery, undulating-edged plates.

BELOW LEFT AND RIGHT: The right ambience lighting is always a favorite thing in any setting—especially in a formal one.

Live and spent foliage gathered on-site are the bulk of this large arrangement. When a breeze is blowing, the candle drips flow down the sides and to the table. It reminds me of fairy-tale stalactites.

INSPIRED
FLORALS

FOLLOW YOUR MUSE

We all have muses of different kinds—people, places, things, to say it simply. And two of mine that inspire creativity are flowers and France.

While wandering in Paris with my husband, we were drawn into a small flower shop that had buckets of the most perfect peonies. Though we were staying just a few more days, I could not resist bringing a couple bunches of my favorite flower back to our apartment. The view of the sparkling Eiffel Tower as backdrop to those pretty pink peonies on the bistro table of our balcony brought two of my muses together in a moment that made a lovely lasting memory.

Beautiful blooms are always talking to me, and gathering a gorgeous mix of flowers and greens for an arrangement is one of my passions. Planning those "flower moments" for my home and gatherings, then picking the blooms and greenery, inhaling their scent, and arranging them together in a container gives me a thrill.

Creating detailed arrangements can seem a bit daunting, but I believe you don't need a formal class to be able to put your bouquet together. There is not a perfect number of stems or by-the-book directions that you need to follow. It is a matter of personal preference, and if you focus on creating a bouquet that makes you smile when you look at it, you can't go wrong.

When in search of floral inspiration, I often start with a trip to our local flower market and just wander and see what catches my eye. Oftentimes, I am surprised—thinking I know just what I am looking for—when a pretty face pops up that speaks to me and spurs an idea in a different direction.

One of the many beauties of going to the flower market is that there is so much to choose from and there are so many possibilities for creating the arrangements of your dreams that you don't have to go in with a detailed list in mind. Which is often better: you can peruse, shop what is in season, and maybe discover a flower that is new to you and start there.

Colorwise, I usually favor blushes, pale creams and whites, and muted peaches, but sometimes what stops me in my tracks are rich, earthy, moody colors. While I love the mix and mingle of various flowers and greenery together, one of my favorite types of bouquets year-round is a monochromatic arrangement of a single seasonal flower. A full bouquet of a single type of bloom in a chunky bucket or basket makes me euphoric. Peonies, lilacs, garden roses, etc., make gorgeous, full arrangements for the table. For small settings, the single-color flower idea works as well, with just a few stems in multiple smaller vessels with nothing else added to them, scattered on the table or placed around the house to extend the color scheme.

We are lucky that our local flower market is known for having some of the best selections year-round, which means I definitely don't have a hard time finding the next flower to fall in love with, even while picking up my most-loved varieties. Many wholesale flower markets open to the trade in the early morning for businesses to shop and then will open their doors to the public mid-morning. So, if you don't have a retail license, you can usually shop without any trouble. My best tip is to get there as early as they will let you shop; many of the vendors close quite early in the day, and if you wait, you might miss them.

If you don't have a wholesale flower market close by, it is a good idea to explore your local florists and shops and find one that seems a good fit for your needs. If you have a good relationship with a retail flower shop, they might also be willing to pick up special-order cut flowers for you upon request when doing their shopping.

The world of beautiful blooms absolutely inspires me, and I feel that flowers are an essential layer of ambience to pay attention to when creating an inspired gathering.

A few of my favorites:

Anemones—So many lovely colors to choose from.

Lilacs—A mix of pale and dark purples and whites.

Ranunculus—In shades of pink, muted oranges, and whites.

Cloni ranunculus—Incredible barely blush color; has larger heads and more ruffles.

Juliet garden roses—This David Austin variety has oodles of layers and a cup shape that opens slowly over several days. (Order slightly ahead to allow them time to open before a party.)

Garden roses and spray roses—I pick up armfuls based on color and scent for mixing.

Peonies—Barely blushing whites and coral ones that fade to a muted peach are my faves, though I don't think I have met a peony that I didn't love.

Dahlias—A spectrum of colors—rich and vibrant or incredibly soft and muted, in a variety of shapes and sizes. Sturdy in a bouquet and abundant all summer. I love the muted Cafe Au Lait, peachy oranges, and a few rich maroons.

Wildflower ranunculus—My newest love, especially the pale variety with a tinge of rosy blush; long-lasting.

Lavender—Lovely to scent a room by itself or added to even the smallest of bouquets.

Greenery—Seeded baby and round eucalyptus, lemon leaf, and olive are my usual staples.

Herbs—Wonderful fragrance boosters for tucking in here and there; my picks are rosemary, lemon thyme, and mint.

My list is always growing and depends somewhat on the season. My best advice is to see which blooms speak to you and start there—you can't go wrong.

I tend to keep roses and peonies a tad bit longer, letting them droop a bit and enjoying them as they drop petals.

Assembling a Bouquet

When creating a bouquet—unless I am going with all one flower—I generally begin with greenery. I find that a good place to start is right outside your door or in the garden. I love to incorporate herbs and fresh clippings of grasses and plants from the surroundings

Next, I add some of the full and prominent blooms to fill the bouquet; in this one, it was peonies and garden roses. This occasion lent itself to a pop of moody color, so I also chose rich burgundy/chocolate with ranunculus and hellabores and oranges with the dahlias.

For height, I favor adding stems of larkspur and delphinium. For drape, I tuck in vines such as jasmine and amaranth; hellebores also vine out in a bouquet and help to add more drape.

For a light airy look, Queen Anne's lace is my choice, and for fullness, I'm taken with lilacs, hydrangeas, peonies, and garden roses in various sizes.

Ranunculus

Peony

Grape Leaves

Juliet Garden Rose

Ranunculus

Dahlia

Peony

White Larkspur

Hellabore

Dahlia

Chocolate Queen Anne's Lace

CREDITS

UNDER THE OAK TREE
Vintage chairs—Bella Cottage
Farm table—built by family
China, table, chair linens—The French Country
    Cottage Market
String lights—Balsam Hill

CHIC BARN CELEBRATION
Star barn—Little Cottage Company
Italian pottery, antique draper's table, antique
    chairs—Eloquence
Chandelier—"Schonbek" from Lamps Plus
Antique chairs—Bella Cottage

DINING ROOM CASUAL LUNCH
Vintage cane chairs—Bella Cottage
Antique French cupboard, pottery, crocks—
    Eloquence
Farm table—made by family
Slipcovers—French Country Cottage Market
Flatware, breadboards—vintage

HARVEST TABLE
My brother's home in Wine Country
Farm table—vintage
Glasses—vintage
Breadboards—HomeGoods

BACKYARD GLAMPING
Chairs—Thos. Baker
Fire pit, lantern, trees, lights—Balsam Hill

FLOWER MEADOW PICNIC
Vintage crate, bottle, pillows—HomeGoods

A TABLE IN THE WOODS
Table, chairs—vintage
Lace plates, gold flatware—Arte Italica
Wood slice serving board—HomeGoods
Velvet linens—French Country Cottage Market

APPLE ORCHARD PIE SOCIAL
Bierwagen's Donner Trail Fruit and Farm Market
Table—Bella Cottage
Chairs—vintage
Velvet chair—vintage
Bucket- vintage

VINEYARD FORMAL
HammerSky Vineyards, Paso Robles, CA
Cane chairs—vintage
Bamboo chairs and tables—HammerSky Vineyards
Plates—Arte Italica

PRIVATE BEACH PARTY
Sling chairs, vintage-style umbrella—
    Business & Pleasure Co.
Cushions, pillows, blankets, galvanized vase—
    HomeGoods
Dishes—Arte Italica
Wine goblets—vintage and new
Flatware—vintage

SUMMER FIELDS GATHERING
Chairs—vintage
Table—Bella Cottage

FLOWERS
San Francisco Flower Market
Safeway
Farmers markets

ACKNOWLEDGMENTS

To my family—you are my biggest inspirations. To my husband—thank you for believing in me, supporting me in all my crazy ideas, and for carrying chairs, tables, flowers, and everything else all over California in your truck. I could not have gotten this book done without you. And to my children—Ryan, Cullan and Ansley—thank you for all the help behind the scenes and for inspiring me every day.

Thank you to my mom, grandmothers, great-grandmothers, and our family, who all showed that creating special moments and memories are the best part of any gathering.

To my dad, Scott, Taylor, and Evan for encouraging me; Chris and family for letting us photograph the vineyard, and my nieces, Elodie and Willa, for helping me.

To Jill Cohen, thank you for believing in me and for your help with bringing *Inspired Gatherings* to print. To Madge Baird, thank you for keeping me on track and for all of your support and patience while I worked. Thank you to designer Rita Sowins and the many folks at Gibbs Smith who helped make it come together so beautifully.

To Michelle at The Bella Cottage, thank you for being such a good friend and your help with perfect pieces.

To Eloquence, thank you for your friendship, for your support of both of my books, and for helping me to add some Eloquence magic to French Country Cottage.

To my Balsam Hill family, thank you for always supporting and encouraging everything I do.

To HomeGoods, Soft Surroundings, Lamps Plus, Arte Italica, thank you for your help with this book.

Special thanks to Little Cottage Company for your help with our barn build.

And to Adam, Luba, and Bev, thank you for your support and friendship.

I am grateful for the beautiful places that inspired us and the people who allowed us to come, make messes with flower petals, set up on their properties, and take photos. Thanks to Melanie and HammerSky Vineyards, Chris and Bierwagen Donner Trail Fruit, Chris and Calypso Vineyards, and to Paris Perfect for a beautiful room with a view in Paris.

To my *French Country Cottage* friends and community—I am so grateful for you. Thank you for taking time out of your day to read, for your notes and kindness, and for your support of my book and *French Country Cottage* always.

ABOUT THE AUTHOR

Courtney founded the lifestyle blog and brand *French Country Cottage*—a place inspired by renovations of her 1940s cottage and about living a lifestyle that is fueled by inspiration. She loves the quintessential mix of rustic and elegant elements—such as an opulent chandelier against weathered wood—indulges a love of all things infused with ambience, and believes that a chandelier and bouquets of fresh flowers belong in every room.

In addition to working as a blogger, she works freelance as a photographer, stylist, and designer. Her first book, *French Country Cottage*, was published in 2018, and her work has been featured in magazines and websites in the US and Europe.

A mom of three grown children, Courtney lives in a little slice of the countryside in California with her husband and dog, Sweet Pea. She loves to travel and discover new inspirations, and you can often find her, camera in hand, playing with flowers. Connect with Courtney on her blog, frenchcountrycottage.net, and on Facebook and Instagram at French Country Cottage.

First Edition
24 23 22 21 20   5 4 3 2 1

Published by
Gibbs Smith
P.O. Box 667
Layton, Utah 84041

1.800.835.4993 orders
www.gibbs-smith.com

Designed by Rita Sowins / Sowins Design
Printed and bound in China

Gibbs Smith books are printed on either recycled, 100% post-consumer waste, FSC-certified
papers or on paper produced from sustainable PEFC-certified forest/controlled wood source.
Learn more at www.pefc.org.

Library of Congress Control Number: 2019949278
ISBN: 978-1-4236-5359-2